My farm jobs

Written by Bronwyn Tainui
Illustrated by Giampietro Costa

raintree
a Capstone company — publishers for children

Mum, Dad and I have a farm. We keep sheep, cows, alpacas and pigs on the farm. We keep ducks and hens, as well.

If they are ill, we get a vet to check on them. Being a vet on a farm is a good job. There is a lot to do on a farm, so I have jobs, too.

We have lots of sheep on the farm. One of my jobs is to check that the sheep are all right. Sheep's tails can get bugs in them, and then the sheep can get sick. I check the sheep's wool coats, too. Wool has a bit of oil in it, so the sheep do not get too wet in the rain. If the wool gets thick, the sheep get too hot. So we shear off the sheep's thick wool in summer. But that is not my job!

On the farm we keep six big cows. My job is to check that no cows are hurt or seem sick. I sing to the cows so that they can hear that I am near. They all look at me. They all look good!

A cow's foot is a hoof. A hoof is hard.

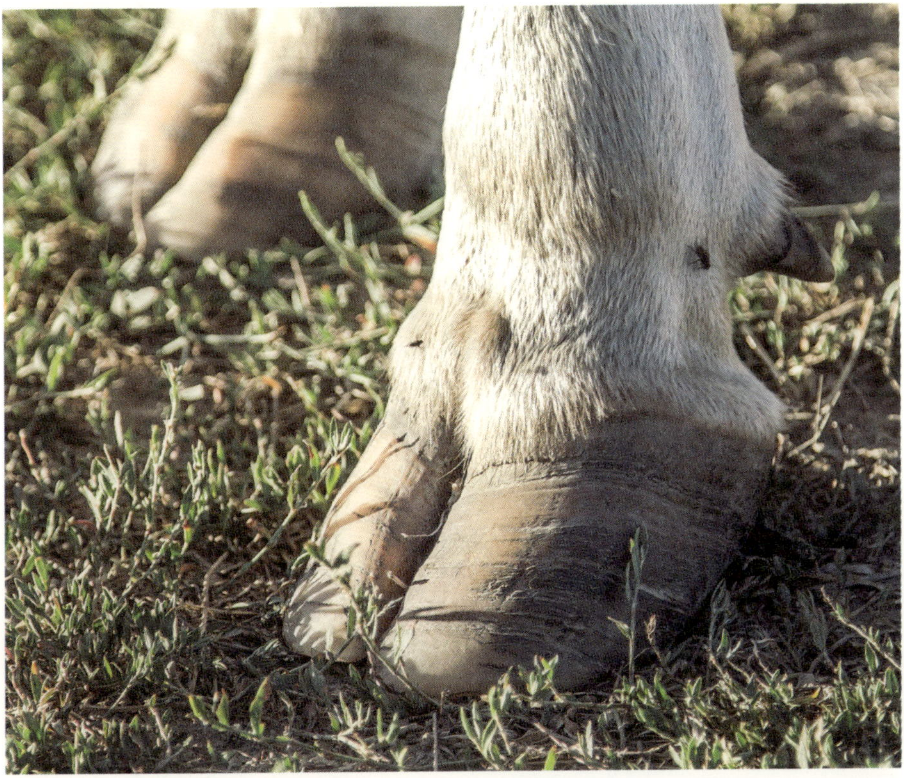

A farmer will cut a cow's hoof if it is too long. Cows do not feel pain in the hoof.

A river runs near the farm. In the morning, the ducks run down to the river. Ducks' wings and backs have a coating of oil, so the ducks can sit on the river without getting too wet. The ducks quack if they see me with a tub of corn. I toss the corn to them. That's my job!

We have a duck coop on the farm. As it gets dark, the ducks hop into the coop. They have a bed there for the night.

I check on the alpacas. I see if I can pat them. The alpacas look as if they might run off, but then they see that I have a bucket of oats. I feed the oats to them. Oats are good for an alpaca.

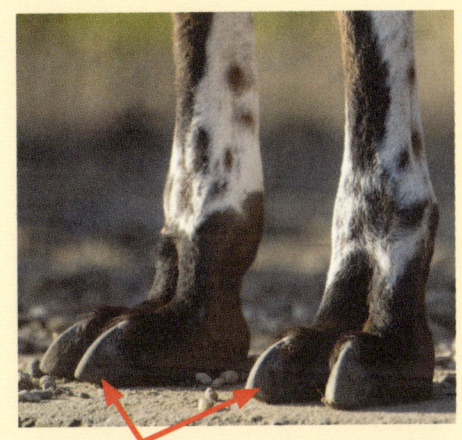

An alpaca's foot has nails. It has a pad on the bottom. It is not a hoof.

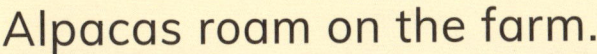

An alpaca's nails

Alpacas roam on the farm.

I feed the pigs on the farm, too. The pigs run up to meet me. I have a big mix of food for them. The mixed-up food looks a mess to me, but they seem to think it is good.

If pigs are hot, mud is good. A dip in mud cools them down. They are a mess!

A mum pig sings to her piglets. I sing to the piglets, too.

Pigs are good fun.

We have lots of hens on the farm. It is my job to pick up the hens' eggs for Mum and Dad. It will be eggs for dinner!

The hens run to me if they see a tub of food. I toss the seed on the soil for them. The hens peck at it. Feeding the hens is my job, too.

At night I shut the hens in the hen coop. They will nap in the coop until the morning.

I tap my leg and yell for my dog, "Max!"

Max and I go for a run. Max barks and wags his tail. We run up the hills. We run on and on, along the farm roads. It is good for dogs to run. They need it. It is fun for me, as well.

We huff and puff. It is hot! I sit on the rocks by the river and dip my feet in. Max hops in. This is a good thing for him to do. Now, he is not so hot.

My cat, Coach, is big with a thick coat of fur. Cats shed fur in the summer, so the coat gets thinner. This is so cats do not get too hot. We do not shear cats! Coach is sitting on a tin roof in the sun. Max barks and Coach hops down to meet us.

Woof!

It is my job to feed her dinner. I pat her and she rubs by my leg.

Coach has a bed in my room at night. If a cat is out in the dark, she might get into a cat fight.

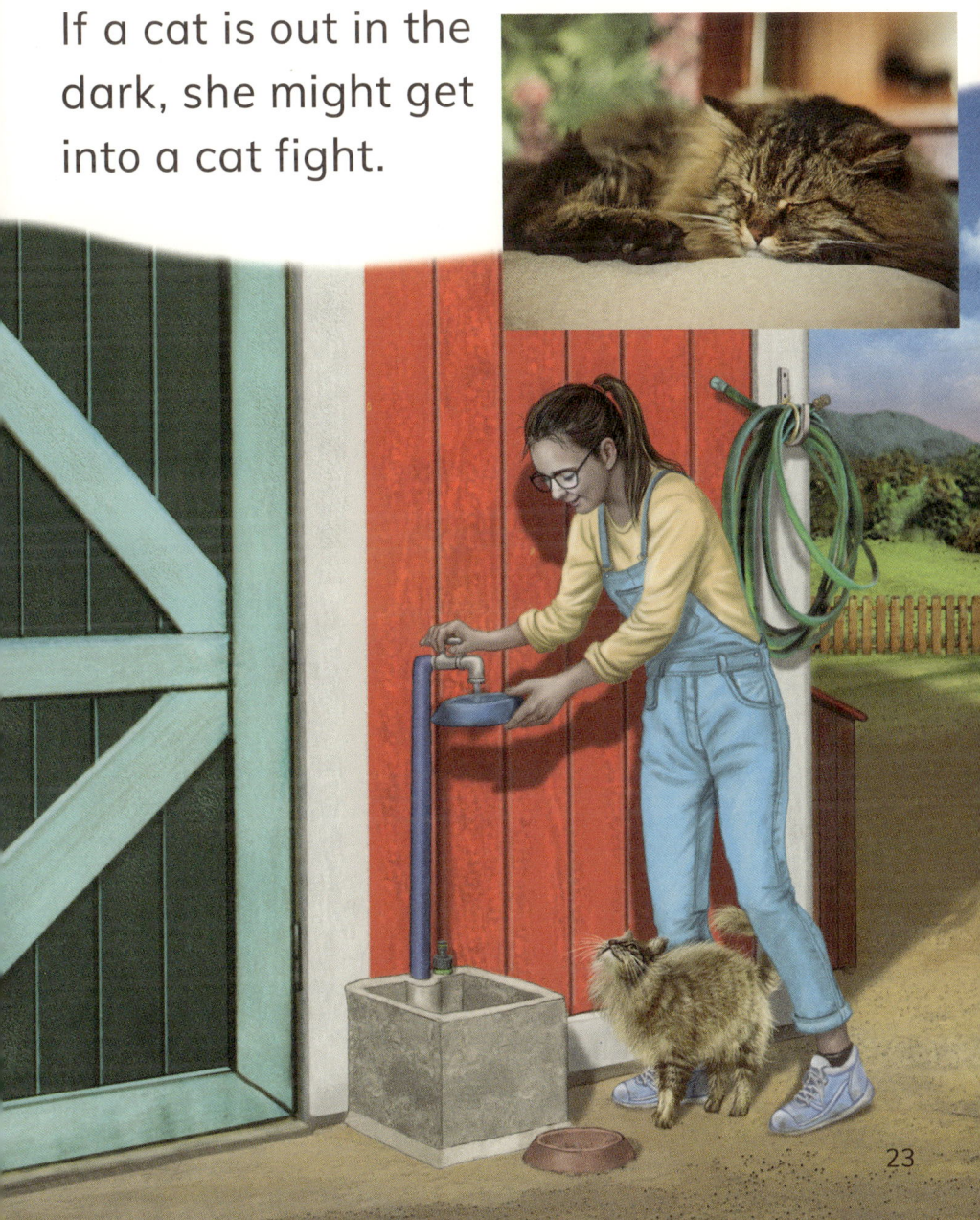

I pick Coach up and tap my leg for Max. I will go back for dinner with Mum and Dad now.

I have finished all my jobs.

Good night!